Justice Beyond The Hague
Supporting the Prosecution
of International Crimes in National Courts

COUNCIL *on*
FOREIGN
RELATIONS

Council Special Report No. 61
June 2011

David A. Kaye

Justice Beyond The Hague
Supporting the Prosecution
of International Crimes in National Courts

Mixed Sources
Product group from well-managed forests and other controlled sources
www.fsc.org   Cert no. SW-COC-001530
© 1996 Forest Stewardship Council

FSC

Contents

Foreword

When the International Criminal Tribunal for the former Yugoslavia (ICTY) was established nearly twenty years ago, the international community had little experience prosecuting the perpetrators of genocide, war crimes, and other atrocities. Unfortunately, there has been ample opportunity to build expertise in the intervening decades; ad hoc tribunals have been established to address past crimes in Cambodia and Sierra Leone, and a formal International Criminal Tribunal for Rwanda (ICTR) was convened in the aftermath of Rwanda's 1994 genocide. Since 2002, the International Criminal Court (ICC) has assumed responsibility for new prosecutions, pursuing war criminals in countries unable or unwilling to bring them to justice domestically.

Yet, after nearly two decades of experience, the limits of these courts' capabilities are becoming clear. While they have brought some senior leaders to justice, the scope of the courts' budgets and their inquiries can never reach all—or even most—perpetrators of atrocities. They are physically far removed from the scenes of the crimes they are prosecuting, cannot compel evidence or conduct independent investigations, and are vulnerable to changes in funding and international political support.

To overcome these and other difficulties, the international community must place greater emphasis on strengthening the national justice systems of the countries where atrocities have occurred. In this Council Special Report, David Kaye examines existing international justice mechanisms, analyzes how they have succeeded and where they have failed, and explains what reforms national legal systems will require to secure just and peaceful outcomes. Cognizant of the myriad individual challenges facing countries experiencing or emerging from violent conflict, Kaye nevertheless identifies a core set of common needs: political pressure on governments reluctant to prosecute perpetrators; assistance in building legal frameworks and training legal officials;

support for investigations, including forensic analysis and security sector reform; and creating belief in the justice system among the local population.

To these ends, Kaye outlines several recommendations for U.S. policymakers and their governmental and nongovernmental partners worldwide. Beginning in the United States, Kaye argues that Washington should expand diplomatic and financial support for national justice systems and appoint a senior official to oversee initiatives from the State Department, Justice Department, USAID, and other agencies. Abroad, he calls for the secretary of state to organize a donor conference to agree on funding priorities and responsibilities for the international community, and to establish a coordinating body to ensure that support for national-level justice systems is properly coordinated and informed by best practices.

Justice Beyond The Hague provides important insights into the strengths and limitations of current international justice mechanisms. It makes a clear case for increasing support to national legal systems and outlines a variety of ways that the U.S. government can improve and coordinate its aid with others. While there will always be a place for international courts in countries that cannot or will not prosecute perpetrators themselves, this Council Special Report successfully argues that domestic systems can and should play a more meaningful role.

Richard N. Haass
President
Council on Foreign Relations
June 2011

Acknowledgments

Authors of Council on Foreign Relations special reports enjoy the privilege of working with a remarkable number of experts from around the country. My experience was no different, and I owe many people thanks. The concept of this report emerged from several conversations with the codirectors of CFR's program on international justice, Matthew C. Waxman and John B. Bellinger III; I am grateful to both Matt and John for the energy they devoted to seeing the report to completion and their careful, detailed comments and advice at every stage. Gideon Copple, research associate at CFR, provided expert research, editing, and advice. I owe a special thanks to CFR President Richard N. Haass and Director of Studies James M. Lindsay for their support and insights as this report approached publication. I am indebted to Patricia Dorff, Lia Norton, and Elias Primoff of CFR's publications department for careful editing and shepherding through to the report's release.

This project gave me the opportunity to spend time with several giants in the field of international justice. The Honorable Thomas Buergenthal, most recently the American judge on the International Court of Justice but a longtime hero to human rights lawyers everywhere—not to mention a dear friend and mentor—provided wisdom and guidance as chair of the advisory committee. The committee itself brought together some of the most thoughtful and influential individuals working in international justice today. I'm especially grateful to those members who participated in our two advisory committee meetings, provided me with a rich assortment of comments and their own work in the field, or discussed with me separately the issues this report raises. Many others in the U.S. government, international organizations, and nongovernmental organizations provided valuable insights and information on background. Larry Johnson, formerly of the UN's Office of Legal Affairs, provided excellent comments on an early draft. This report was made possible by the support of the John D. and Catherine

T. MacArthur Foundation as part of its broader grant to the CFR program on international justice, and I owe a special thanks to Mary Page and Eric Sears of MacArthur.

Much as I relied on the advice of so many in the field of international justice, the views expressed in this report are my own, and I take responsibility for any errors or omissions it may contain.

David A. Kaye

Council Special Report

Introduction

For nearly two decades, the United Nations has created international criminal tribunals to punish those responsible for war crimes, crimes against humanity, and genocide. Since the early 1990s the United States has strongly supported the UN tribunals for Rwanda and the former Yugoslavia and hybrid UN/national courts for Sierra Leone and Cambodia. The era of court-building culminated in the 1998 adoption, over U.S. objections, of a treaty to establish a permanent International Criminal Court (ICC) in The Hague. These international courts have brought dozens of perpetrators to justice, and the UN Security Council's requests that the ICC investigate the situations in Sudan (2005) and Libya (2011) show that policymakers across the spectrum, in the United States and abroad, believe that accountability—that is, bringing individuals to justice for committing atrocities—can be an important tool to combat war crimes, crimes against humanity, and genocide. Yet as important as these courts are, atrocities occur in places beyond their reach, and even where international courts investigate and prosecute, they lack the capacity to try all but a handful of the thousands of perpetrators of the worst international crimes.[1]

Given the limitations of international courts, policymakers and advocates—within governments, multilateral organizations, and nongovernmental organizations (NGOs)—increasingly recognize the need to help build justice at *national* levels. National-level justice is closer to the communities that most need it; it does not merely fill the gaps left by international courts. It penalizes the worst kind of governance, removing and stigmatizing civilian and military officials responsible for widespread and systematic abuses. Achieving justice for war crimes and other atrocities can also help restore political and economic stability in postconflict societies.

In its 2011 *World Development Report*, the World Bank concluded that postconflict justice at national levels—criminal prosecutions, truth and reconciliation commissions, national inquiries, and the like—play an important role in rebuilding institutions necessary for security, stability, and economic development. In transitional political situations, criminal accountability can "send powerful signals about the commitment of the new government to the rule of law."[2] Not all of these goals are attainable at all times; politics and dynamics pitting justice against peace sometimes get in the way, and efforts to build institutions capable of conducting war crimes investigations and prosecutions take time to develop.[3] Still, justice for perpetrators of atrocities contributes to stability—a first step toward the development of institutions that are responsive to a country's citizens.

The Democratic Republic of Congo (DRC) illustrates the vast effort required to provide national justice and the risks of failing to support it. Government, nonstate, and foreign forces in the Congo committed massive atrocities beginning in 1993.[4] The ICC is investigating a tiny fraction of those responsible. Most perpetrators escape ICC justice because of the court's focus on prosecuting senior officials, but also because it may only investigate crimes committed after July 2002, when the Rome Statute, which created the ICC, entered into force. The DRC's own domestic courts, if capable, should step in to handle the vast majority of crimes. However, because the DRC lacks the law, the courts, the prisons—in short, the necessary legal and physical infrastructure—it needs external support to hold perpetrators accountable and begin rebuilding rule of law. If left unchecked, the gravity of those crimes—rape, murder, and pillage on a massive scale—will spell a future of continuing lawlessness, further undermining stability in an already unstable, resource-rich part of the world. While many governmental and multilateral donors work to support justice in the DRC, their efforts are at the early stages, and they lack the coordination and long-term commitment necessary to build credible justice institutions there.[5]

With respect to the crisis in Libya, national accountability should also play a role in the long-term building of a post-Qaddafi regime. The UN Security Council referral for ICC investigation, focused on ending the Qaddafi regime's violence against civilians, will have a short-term impact. At best, it could encourage defections from the regime and further isolate its leadership, with the optimal result of Muammar al-Qaddafi's departure from power and subsequent trial; at worst, it could harden the resolve of regime leaders to prevail over opposition forces and remain in power, thereby avoiding the humiliation of a trial in The Hague.[6] A post-Qaddafi national process in Libya—in which those responsible for the regime's crimes are held responsible—will be more likely than Hague-based justice to reconcile opposing forces and facilitate an environment conducive to building new governing institutions. Even now, Libyan and international actors should lay the groundwork for such national mechanisms.

The United States should support the efforts of national courts to hold accountable those accused of war crimes, crimes against humanity, and genocide. Governments and multilateral organizations have begun to turn their attention to national-level justice, but, as in the DRC, their efforts lack the coordination and commitment needed to make a real difference to nations in the midst of or emerging from conflict. A major question facing policymakers is how to harness the energy and resources that they previously mobilized to set up international tribunals and apply those lessons to build the infrastructure for domestic courts, which can then be used to prosecute war crimes and crimes against humanity at the national level.

The United States should put national-level justice at the center of its war crimes policy. Internally, the United States should reorganize how it helps other governments develop the capacity to investigate and prosecute such crimes. It should identify a senior official to coordinate U.S. efforts and find cost-effective (as well as cost-neutral) ways to improve American support for national justice. Externally, the United States should take a leading role in fixing and coordinating a currently dysfunctional international approach to national justice in the wake of atrocities. By taking these steps, the United States will ensure that national courts play a central role in stability and nation-building in regions of conflict, laying new foundations that are closely aligned to U.S. security and development interests.

The Universe of International Justice

The United States and other governments, multilateral organizations, and NGOs should aim to help make national courts effective venues for the prosecution of mass human rights abuses. A number of actors, nationally and internationally, facilitate investigations and prosecutions of serious international crimes. Policymakers should mobilize these actors and institutions to support the ability of national courts to pursue such difficult cases.

NATIONAL INSTITUTIONS

Countries as varied as Argentina, Bosnia, Colombia, and Germany, among many others, have established national processes to hold their citizens accountable for war crimes and crimes against humanity. Some countries create special judicial chambers to try perpetrators, as occurred in Bosnia, while others establish prosecutorial posts to specialize in atrocities, as in Argentina. Many countries, including the members of NATO, insist on trying their military personnel accused of war crimes in military courts, even while providing their civilian courts with war crimes jurisdiction.

There are good reasons to support prosecutions at national levels. According to the World Bank, national-level justice contributes to "legitimate institutions and governance" that are "crucial to break cycles of violence."[7] National-level prosecutions help educate communities about past conflict and foster support for rule of law. They create cadres of professionals who learn how to manage complex cases against people in power. However, national prosecutions also face difficult political issues. If seen as corrupt, biased, inconsistent, or inept, national efforts undermine faith in the rule of law, heighten domestic tensions, and reignite conflict. Many governments lack the resources required for all the facets of legitimate justice: fair and humane polic- ing, investigations, and witness protection programs; independent judges of character and probity; prosecutors making choices widely seen as lawful and just; defense counsel capable of serving their clients' best interests; outreach and education and the broad public buy-in that comes with them; and strong governmental support.

Governments often face difficult choices in dealing with past crimes.[8] For instance, the first postapartheid government in South Africa feared that an immediate turn to criminal prosecutions would sow discord at a time when it wanted to move beyond racial violence and rebuild a state. It adopted a Truth and Reconciliation Commission in which political crimes were the subject of amnesties so long as their perpetrators told the truth about those acts. East Timor has combined criminal trials with truth and reconciliation approaches.[9] Colombia adopted a Justice and Peace Law that emphasizes normalization and demobilization pro- cesses even while authorizing criminal investigations and prosecutions. Other countries have adopted commissions of inquiry that lead to the removal of public officials from office. Rwanda modified traditional local methods of conflict resolution to create the *gacaca* process in the wake of the 1994 genocide.[10] If implemented in good faith, these kinds of noncriminal approaches supplement and eventually assist a transi- tion to criminal justice.

Domestic NGOs often play pivotal roles in national justice. For example, some lawyers and human rights leaders in Colombia are push- ing the government to hold war crimes perpetrators accountable. They document abuses, lobby the government, litigate on behalf of civilian victims, and provide education and access to justice, particularly in rural areas far from metropolitan centers like Bogotá.[11]

INTERNATIONAL COURTS

In 1993, following widespread atrocities in Bosnia, the UN Security Council established the International Criminal Tribunal for the former Yugoslavia (ICTY) in The Hague, triggering a decade of multilateral court building.[12] When, a year later, ethnic Hutus slaughtered hun- dreds of thousands of Tutsis in Rwanda, the Security Council created the International Criminal Tribunal for Rwanda (ICTR), locating it in Arusha, Tanzania.[13] The Security Council directed both so-called ad hoc tribunals to prosecute war crimes, crimes against humanity, and genocide. During this period of court building, the United Nations convened governments and NGOs to establish a permanent international criminal court with global jurisdiction. These negotiations led to a treaty creating the ICC. The Rome Statute, concluded in Rome during the summer of 1998, was created over the objections of the Clinton administration and Congress.[14] By 2003, the ICC opened its offices in The Hague. Negotiators of the Rome Statute, after U.S. prompting, built in a preference for domestic justice: the ICC may exercise jurisdiction only where the relevant domestic actors are unwilling or unable to do so. Unlike the ICTY and ICTR, which had primacy over national courts for war crimes issues, the ICC *complements* national-level justice systems by coming into play only when those national-level systems fail to investigate or prosecute in good faith. In grave situations where national-level justice seems futile, the UN Security Council has referred investigations to the ICC, as it did for Sudan over Darfur and for Libya.[15]

International courts face significant constraints. They operate far from the scenes of the crimes and lack the resources to hold more than a handful of senior officials accountable for atrocities.[16] They lack police forces of their own so they cannot compel evidence and apprehend suspects; governments of alleged perpetrators typically fail to cooperate, and foreign governments, even strong supporters of international justice, normally resist using force to arrest fugitives.[17] They rarely, if ever, succeed in reconciling formerly warring communities.[18] In short, the success of international tribunals depends on governmental efforts that do not always materialize.

Notwithstanding these constraints, the UN tribunals have brought to justice dozens of senior officials, civilian and military, who conceived, planned, and otherwise helped commit atrocities. They have shaped international law and brought justice to the top of domestic and international agendas. For instance, Serbia, Croatia, and Bosnia have developed the capacity to conduct domestic war crimes investigations and prosecutions as a result of the ICTY and U.S. and EU pressure.[19] ICC investigations have triggered national investigations in places as diverse as Kenya, the DRC, and Colombia.[20]

HYBRID AND INTERNATIONALIZED DOMESTIC COURTS

The United Nations has also established hybrid tribunals in which international and domestic investigators, prosecutors, judges, defense counsel, and other judicial sector professionals try criminal cases together.[21] The Special Court for Sierra Leone, based in Freetown since 2002, and the Extraordinary Chambers in the Courts of Cambodia (also known as the Khmer Rouge Tribunal), based in Phnom Penh since 2006, bring together international and domestic personnel and law in single institutions, prosecuting the most senior officials responsible for atrocities, such as former Liberian president Charles Taylor and the leading associates of Khmer Rouge leader Pol Pot. The Special War Crimes Chamber of the Bosnian state court is fully established within the Bosnian legal system but brings international civil servants to serve roles as prosecutors, defense lawyers, judges, investigators, and court managers. UN administrators have established similar hybrid national/international courts in Kosovo and East Timor.[22] Outside the area of war crimes and crimes against humanity, the UN Security Council has created the Special Tribunal for Lebanon to investigate and prosecute those responsible for the assassination of former Lebanese prime minister Rafiq Hariri and related terrorism.

The hybrid tribunals inject international expertise and resources into situations badly in need of both. Like national courts, however, they face political obstacles. The Cambodian government has repeatedly sought inappropriate political influence over the Khmer Rouge Tribunal.[23] The Bosnian war crimes chamber has the support of the Bosnian Muslim and Croat communities, but not of Bosnian Serbs. They have uneven records integrating into domestic systems, typically not triggering broader reconstruction of law enforcement and judicial institutions.

REGIONAL COURTS AND COMMISSIONS

Regional organizations have established human rights courts to help promote international standards in their domestic legal systems. These courts are not criminal tribunals, but they do allow individuals—often with the support of human rights organizations—to appeal to them when their governments fail to observe human rights obligations. With its forty-seven member states, the Council of Europe's European Court for Human Rights is the most prominent and successful example. It has also promoted the pursuit of justice at the national level.[24] The Organization of American States' Inter-American Court for Human Rights, with jurisdiction over twenty-five states in the Americas (not including the United States and Canada), has helped encourage the development and use of domestic mechanisms in Colombia, Argentina, Guatemala, and elsewhere.[25] Regional mechanisms in Africa—the African Commission on Human and People's Rights, the East African Court of Justice, and the Economic Community of West African States (ECOWAS) Court of Justice—and in Asia are at early stages of attempting to develop similar roles in their own environments.[26] Regional courts offer advantages that international bodies cannot always provide: proximity to countries in conflict, for example, or an understanding of local trends and legal cultures as well as personnel with strong ties to national legal institutions.

UN BODIES

Several institutions within the UN system investigate alleged atrocities, report on their findings, recommend further investigation and prosecution, and otherwise trigger international action before, during, and after conflict. UN peacekeeping forces increasingly support accountability efforts; the United Nations Organization Stabilization Mission in the Democratic Republic of the Congo (MONUSCO), for instance, supports mobile courts in the east of the country, bringing judges to otherwise remote crime scenes to address crimes of sexual violence.[27] The UN High Commissioner for Human Rights, UN special rapporteurs, and ad hoc fact-finding missions provide detailed information on abuses, usually through reports to UN political bodies.[28] The Human Rights Council, whose work is often highly politicized, may draw attention to atrocities through votes to censure governmental behavior.[29] Treaty bodies outside the UN system—such as the Human Rights Committee of the International Covenant on Civil and Political Rights and the Committee Against Torture of the Convention Against Torture—collect information that, like all of these institutions, can feed into national efforts and spur local, regional, or international actors to investigate and prosecute abuses.

INTEGRATING ACCOUNTABILITY MECHANISMS

The courts and investigative mechanisms described above occasionally share information, but their work is not well integrated. The ICTY transferred evidence collected during its investigations to support prosecutions by the Sarajevo War Crimes Chamber. The UN's Darfur Commission of Inquiry in 2004 collected substantial amounts of information as part of its work, which was then provided to the ICC prosecutor. Officials from international and hybrid courts participate in short-term training sessions for national-level prosecutors, defense counsel, judges, and court managers. They do not, however, collaborate on core strategic issues such as the selection of defendants or the choice of crimes to investigate. American policymakers, working with partners in foreign governments, international organizations, and NGOs, should work to integrate national and international mechanisms to build or improve accountability at national levels.

What Domestic Systems Need to Succeed

THE SPECTRUM OF NATIONAL CHALLENGES

No two national systems present the same set of challenges.[30] They vary significantly in terms of political will, from governments that seek support for national prosecutions to ones that reject any form of justice, at international or domestic levels. They vary in stages of development, from those with strong preexisting legal systems to those decimated by conflict.

At one end of the spectrum, governments like Bosnia's work with the international community to build criminal justice for international crimes. Bosnia's postwar international institution responsible for implementing the Dayton Peace Accords, the Office of the High Representative, created a special domestic Bosnian war crimes chamber in the Bosnian state court system, to which some ICTY cases involving less senior indictees could be transferred. The United States and the European Union provided funding in 2004 to launch the chamber. The chamber involves international and national prosecutors and investigators, transitioning to make the chamber a purely domestic institution. The chamber tried several transferred cases from the ICTY and launched its own investigations and prosecutions, even though the Bosnian Serb community has resisted its work. The infusion of financial and human capital from the U.S. government and the EU has been essential. Moreover, the chamber's close relationship with the ICTY has enabled the exchange of expertise, information, and personnel.[31]

Further along the spectrum of political will are states that partially commit to accountability, like Colombia, a country riven by a decades-long civil war involving an array of government, insurgent, and paramilitary groups.[32] In 2005, Colombia adopted the Justice and Peace Law, providing for the demobilization of paramilitary forces and the prosecution of those responsible for war crimes. The Justice and Peace

Law provides a limited response to the atrocities committed during the civil war.[33] The Office of the Public Prosecutor, with the support of U.S. lawyers from the Department of Justice, has pursued a handful of cases against paramilitary actors, but the prosecutions have focused on individual crimes rather than systematic criminal activity implicating senior officials.[34] The ICC has been conducting a preliminary investigation in Colombia since 2005, warning that it would initiate a formal investigation if the Colombian government fails to pursue senior officials for wrongdoing.[35] Civil society organizations in Colombia have also filed cases at the Inter-American Court for Human Rights, which has responded by calling for prosecutions by Colombian authorities.[36]

Colombia also provides an example of a country in which some abuses long predate the advent of the ICC, which cannot prosecute crimes committed prior to July 2002. Other countries fall into this category as well—some involving long-ago abuses, such as those during the Bangladesh War in the early 1970s, Cambodia's rule by the Khmer Rouge, and Afghanistan under the Taliban.[37]

International support does not always follow government requests. The first Iraqi government after the American-led invasion in 2003 established the Iraqi High Tribunal to hold senior members of Saddam Hussein's Baath regime accountable for a vast number of atrocities. The United States, and to a lesser extent the United Kingdom, offered significant support to the Iraqi tribunal, as did the International Bar Association and a handful of NGOs. However, the United Nations and most governments refused to provide support; objections to the Iraq invasion, post-invasion governance issues, and due process concerns, among other factors, stood in the way.[38] Regardless of the reasons, the Iraqi criminal process suffered significantly from the lack of foreign support, and its legitimacy is still questioned by NGOs and governments.

A third segment of the spectrum involves ongoing crises, widespread failures of basic elements of security and law, and systematic atrocities, all met by piecemeal responses from the international community. The DRC's problems, for instance, include a largely nonexistent infrastructure; a decimated legal profession; epidemics of massive violence against civilians, especially women and girls; and a vast territory that lacks basic transportation and communication links. The Congolese military has attempted to conduct trials, but the weak military justice system has limited jurisdiction.[39] The United States, the EU, and others support

MONUSCO's mobile courts to prosecute sexual violence, training, and other programs especially to deal with gender-based violence. The ICC, pursuing cases against leaders of local and regional armed groups, has yet to conclude a single trial and does not support local efforts. Neither the Congolese government nor international donors have adopted a strategy to build domestic capacity for prosecutions.[40] The United States and other actors are pressing the DRC to develop a hybrid war crimes chamber in the DRC courts.[41] Even with such a chamber, supporters will face massive resource and education challenges in creating a viable nation-wide system of war crimes accountability.

At the far end of the spectrum are states that refuse to hold any officials accountable. Sudan, for instance, has rejected justice for the atrocities in Darfur. As Sudan is not a party to the ICC, the UN Security Council referred the situation to the ICC prosecutor to investigate (as the Rome Statute permits), with the tacit endorsement of the United States. Since then, the ICC has issued arrest warrants for three senior Sudanese government officials, including President Umar Hassan Ahmad al-Bashir, but none of them has been arrested and the Security Council has provided little support. Adding to the problem, the Arab League and the African Union have stymied efforts to apprehend Bashir.[42]

ELEMENTS OF SUPPORT

Among the instances of national-level investigations and prosecutions, only in Bosnia did international actors—the ICTY, the UN Security Council, the United States, and the EU—systematically coordinate their efforts and provide substantial funding and long-term support. More typically, governments and international organizations do not coordinate their efforts. In addition, support for "accountability"— justice for the most serious, widespread, and systematic human rights violations—often is not connected to more general international efforts to support development of the rule of law at national levels. Rule of law support implies support for law enforcement, legal and judicial training, anticorruption initiatives, and a vast range of other initiatives. Holding perpetrators responsible for mass human rights violations should be seen as part of rule of law development, but it generally proceeds on a different, unrelated track. This compartmentalization of "accountability" and "rule of law" programming means that support for one does not benefit the other, which is counter-productive and a poor use of donor dollars. Support for accountability should be integrated as a central aspect of building rule of law in the wake of conflict.

The kinds of support necessary to building national systems of accountability include the following:

Political incentives: Governments and UN bodies provide modest political support or pressure in favor of prosecutions of war crimes perpetrators. The United States and other Western governments have pressed Bosnia and Colombia, for instance, to pursue domestic justice. The EU conditioned Serbian and Croatian candidacy for membership on the development of domestic rule of law, including accountability.

Legal assistance: Where countries lack a basic legal framework for war crimes prosecutions, foreign governments and NGOs are well-suited to help draft national legislation to provide the legal basis for prosecutions. Pro bono legal groups, NGOs, and law schools in North America and Europe have participated in these kinds of efforts.

Investigative and analytical support: In the face of ongoing conflict or limited infrastructure, it is often too much to ask a government to secure testimony, forensics, and other forms of evidence. The UN Mapping Exercise in the DRC did just that, though, collecting hundreds of documents and interviewing hundreds of witnesses to provide a basis for any future criminal process. With similar aims, Canada, Finland, and the EU have formed Justice Rapid Response, an organization with a roster of experts who may be available to serve that kind of function when national authorities are unavailable.[43]

Security sector reform: Many war-torn or collapsed states lack viable courtrooms, humane or secure detention facilities, and office space for prosecutors, defense counsel, and judges. Moreover, police and other security agencies often fail to provide an environment in which accountability is feasible.[44] Security sector donors provide assistance to build these kinds of capacities. Such donors typically do not link their work to those working on justice for those accused of atrocities, but the fields are closely related and should be better integrated.

Training and education: The international courts and dozens of international NGOs, such as the International Bar Association, the American Bar Association's Rule of Law Initiative, Avocats Sans Frontières, and the Open Society Justice Initiative, support local organizations or train jurists, from prosecutors and defense counsel to judges, police, and witness protection officers. These are typically short-term programs, rather than long-term, sustainable education strategies.[45]

Outreach: International and hybrid courts, sometimes working with NGOs, conduct outreach programs to generate the understanding and support of local populations for justice initiatives.[46] Domestic support minimizes the ability of political actors to manipulate accountability in ways that stir up interethnic conflict. Public understanding helps support the identification of witnesses and can contribute to their protection later in the process. Outreach can also nurture greater public appreciation for the rule of law, due process, and norms of international law.

There is no mystery to what domestic systems generally need to succeed, even if assistance must be tailored to each situation's requirements. The challenge is to provide that assistance in effective, efficient ways.

Global Support for International Justice

To be effective, any program to support justice for atrocities at the national level needs both adequate coordination at the policy and ground levels as well as sufficient financial and technical resources. However, the United States and its international partners are not currently meeting those needs. While limited funding is a substantial barrier, the principal stumbling blocks involve poor coordination among donors and a preference for short-term projects over long-term strategies.

U.S. SUPPORT FOR INTERNATIONAL JUSTICE

At the international level, the United States has been the leading financial and political supporter for the ad hoc UN tribunals. The United States has contributed nearly $1 billion to the ICTY and ICTR combined since 1993 and more than $80 million to the Special Court for Sierra Leone.[47] Traditionally, Congress has provided strong political support of the United Nations and hybrid tribunals. For instance, it conditioned aid to Serbia on Belgrade's cooperation with the ICTY and support to the Khmer Rouge Tribunal on independence from Cambodian governmental interference.[48]

Meanwhile, U.S. support for the ICC has evolved. After a period of hesitation and then open opposition, the United States, beginning in 2005, looked to the ICC as a tool to advance U.S. goals concerning international justice.[49] In 2005, the Bush administration accepted the ICC as the only available institution to investigate and prosecute Sudanese officials for the crimes in Darfur. In 2010, while reiterating that the United States does not plan to become party to the Rome Statute, the Obama administration attended the ICC Review Conference in Kampala. The U.S. National Security Strategy in 2010 expressed support for ICC prosecutions "that advance U.S. interests and values."[50] The Obama administration supported referral of Libya to the ICC in 2011.

Even while helping build international tribunals, the United States has long supported justice at national levels, providing rhetorical—if not always financial—support for accountability in national courts.[51] The 2010 National Security Strategy noted that the United States is "working to strengthen national justice systems."[52] The U.S. departments of State, Defense, Justice, and the U.S. Agency for International Development (USAID) fund or operate modest programs to support accountability abroad, and the Obama administration created a National Security Council post dealing specifically with war crimes and atrocity prevention. Within the State Department, the ambassador-at-large for war crimes issues leads policy development, working with the Office of the Legal Adviser, regional bureaus, special advisers such as the Office for Women's Issues, the Bureau for Democracy, Rights, and Labor, and, for rule of law issues, the Bureau for International Narcotics and Law Enforcement. USAID provides assistance through its democracy and governance division. The war crimes ambassador does not enjoy substantial grant-making or programmatic funds. As a result, although other agencies and bureaus finance some rule of law efforts, the war crimes office must lobby others to support accountability efforts.

The U.S. Department of Justice also trains and supports national prosecutors. For instance, Justice Department lawyers in Baghdad, acting as part of the specially created Regime Crimes Liaison Office, advised the Iraqi High Tribunal.[53] The Defense Department's Defense Institute of International Legal Studies provides training in a military justice context, as it is now doing in the DRC. The Department of Defense's experiences with reconstruction in Afghanistan and Iraq have also provided lessons for the building of rule of law institutions, leading to the creation of a new coordinator for the department's efforts. In 2005, the U.S. government created the Civilian Response Corps, an interagency body designed to draw expertise from throughout the federal government to provide support in postconflict or humanitarian relief situations.

Despite the number of programs, the United States generally supports accountability at national levels in an ad hoc and only modestly resourced way. Occasionally agencies will coalesce around a particular need, such as the present acknowledgment that the DRC needs assistance to hold perpetrators accountable for international crimes, especially sexual and gender-based violence. But even the support for DRC efforts applies only tangentially to war crimes or crimes against humanity. In 2010, Congress appropriated just $15 million for security and humanitarian assistance efforts in the DRC, only a small portion of which goes to accountability for a country approximately the size of Alaska and Texas combined and with an estimated 70 million people.[54] By contrast, the United States and the EU contributed over $30 million to build the war crimes chamber in the Bosnian state court, a much smaller country with a preexisting infrastructure and legal culture.

Even where the United States provides support, U.S. agencies do not coordinate their efforts well. Each agency pursues its own agenda, and no official or office bears responsibility for supporting justice at national levels. The Obama administration already recognizes that coordination problems can undermine development policy.[55] The State Department's December 2010 Quadrennial Diplomacy and Development Review (QDDR) urges agencies to designate officials who can take the lead in the coordination of assistance.[56] Although the QDDR does not address accountability for international crimes, it does call for building "effective and accountable security and justice institutions."[57]

FOREIGN GOVERNMENTS AND INTERNATIONAL ORGANIZATIONS

Other leading governments supporting international justice are, by and large, members of the ICC. They typically support domestic efforts in situations where the ICC is also conducting investigations or prosecutions.[58] Major funders include the European Union, the German development agency GIZ, and Scandinavian governmental actors.[59] For instance, in the DRC, the EU and its member states support police reform, training of magistrates in the civilian and military justice systems, prisons, and civil society development.[60] UN agencies, especially the UN Development Program, provide substantial support to rule of law efforts.[61]

In the field, donors tend toward ad hoc coordination of projects, better in some countries than others. From capitals, however, foreign governments and international organizations generally fail to coordinate, each funding and initiating projects according to their own independent objectives. In 2006, the United Nations established a mechanism to coordinate rule of law funding, the Rule of Law Coordination and Resource Group, but it did not apply to projects aimed at holding responsible perpetrators of mass human rights violations, and it was limited to UN donors. Professionals in rule of law and accountability work believe it would be difficult to extend the UN mechanism to the array of governmental and NGO actors providing support for accountability.[62] The ICC's governing body and its leading officials have made clear that the ICC should not play a coordinating role regarding domestic accountability.[63]

GAPS IN INTERNATIONAL SUPPORT

As the World Bank has noted, governmental donors lack incentives to coordinate because they want independence and need clear success stories to tout to their legislative constituencies.[64] The flip side of independence, however, is costly: either neglect or duplication and failure to develop strategies based upon a country's needs.[65] Particularly as resources are dwindling, coordination would allow donor dollars to go further, creating mechanisms for them to concentrate assistance in those areas where it can make the most difference. The creation of regularized information sharing and joint country approaches would go a long way to improve coordination.

Meanwhile, donors tend to fund programs that are, for the most part, near-term projects, such as short-term training and one-off outreach programs. As important as it is to show short-term benefit, support is largely wasted when it fails to invest in long-term projects. Yet it is difficult to identify any genuinely long-term multilateral efforts apart from the work of the United States and the European Union in building the war crimes chamber in Bosnia—and even there the availability of continued support is uncertain. U.S. Department of Justice support for Colombia's prosecutors, for instance, has been admirably long-term, but it is unconnected to what other American, UN, and European donors are doing in the country. Foreign universities with expertise in international criminal law from time to time hold exchanges with colleagues in postconflict countries, but, with few exceptions, they do not provide the kind of long-term training that benefits local lawyers, judges, and others in the justice sector.

Finally, long-term support means investment of financial and other resources. To date, those resources specifically devoted to justice at the national level have been modest apart from a few examples noted above, particularly in comparison to the hundreds of millions of dollars spent annually on international and hybrid courts. The rhetoric of support for domestic accountability has never been stronger. But a serious push for justice at the national levels, one that will be sustainable and, ultimately, an impetus for improved rule of law and national stability, requires that governments devote the same energy and resources that went into building international courts almost twenty years ago.

Recommendations for U.S. Strategy

Governments and international organizations increasingly recognize a need to support national prosecutions, but a lack of coordination, resources, and long-term programming stands in the way. The U.S. government can and should play a leading role in helping to develop accountability mechanisms for atrocity crimes at the national level. To be sure, the United States faces some constraints: it is not a party to the ICC, and it must deal with widely held perceptions, especially abroad, that it failed to hold its own officials accountable for abuses against suspected terrorism detainees.[66] However, it can contribute and lead by taking advantage of its deep experience as an advocate for justice in the wake of mass atrocities and its distinct convening power to bring together partners already supporting national jurisdictions.

A U.S. strategy for building support for justice at the domestic level should include several initiatives:

The president should issue a Presidential Policy Directive (PPD) to expand and improve coordination of U.S. support of accountability.

Getting agencies to coordinate domestic support will require presidential leadership. A Presidential Policy Directive should provide overall policy guidance to U.S. government agencies on international justice and U.S. cooperation with the ICC, formalizing the periodic policy statements on international justice issues from senior State Department officials and putting in context favorable U.S. policy toward the ICC in places such as northern Uganda and Libya, where international justice is high on the agenda. With respect to national investigations and prosecutions, the PPD should include a statement of how U.S. support for national accountability reflects a long-term investment in rule of law and stability for nations in or emerging from conflict.

The president should appoint a senior official to coordinate support.

The PPD should identify a senior official or particular office as the inter-agency lead for assisting domestic accountability efforts abroad. That official could be based in the staff of the National Security Council—the appropriate location for interagency coordination. Alternatively, the coordinator could be a senior official based in one of the civilian security bureaus proposed in the QDDR, such as under the proposed undersecretary of state for civilian security, democracy, and human rights. The U.S. ambassador-at-large for war crimes issues, who might fall within the new undersecretary's jurisdiction, could be another alternative, provided that the office is granted sufficient authority to coordinate independent sources of funding.[67]

The United States should convene a domestic supporters' conference with members of Congress, philanthropic donors, and NGOs.

Support for national accountability will require a broad base of American backers. The PPD should kick-start the process by setting up a joint public-private mechanism for the support of national accountability efforts. Its first step should involve a conference bringing together the major supporters, and potential supporters, in financial, political, and diplomatic terms. Members of Congress need to be brought in early on as partners, as it will be crucial to develop a constituency of legislators who agree that support for justice is a long-term investment in stability and the rule of law. Beyond bringing legislators into the process, the administration and supporters of national justice also need to vigor-ously and continually make the case that holding perpetrators respon-sible advances postconflict reconstruction and stability operations.

The United States will need to increase its own levels of financial support if it is to become a credible leader on national accountability. Taking as an example the Sarajevo war crimes chamber, which cost more than $30 million, policymakers should expect that costs could be at least that high for each country where a serious effort is made to sup-port national jurisdictions. Of course, seeking increased funding in a time of downsizing budgets and congressional resistance to new spend-ing is not likely to be feasible. The United States and its partners will therefore need to identify opportunities for funding. For instance, as the ICTY and ICTR complete their work, their costs will also decrease substantially; for the first time since their creation, their budgets are already beginning to shrink. The executive branch should work with Congress to shift the funds that previously supported the ICTY and ICTR to justice initiatives at the national level. Moreover, it should encourage other major funders to do the same. Such redirection could amount to tens of millions of dollars annually once these tribunals complete their work.

The public-private partnership should make particular use of American philanthropy. Historically, U.S. philanthropic foundations have been essential to the development of human rights and international justice sectors; many major foundations remain engaged in human rights and international justice.[68] Foundations could convene governmental and nongovernmental actors to develop ideas for broader international support for national accountability.

Working with like-minded countries, the United States should launch an international coordinating body to support national-level justice and accountability.

The United States, working with its partners, should establish a mechanism that would coordinate support among all major actors. A coordinating body for domestic accountability (CODA) should be made up of representatives from donor and recipient governments, international organizations, NGOs, and private philanthropies. It would perform three functions: coordinate strategy, share information concerning donor projects, and serve as a clearinghouse for best practices and country knowledge and experience. In 2009, the United States, United Kingdom, and Canada initiated a similar effort to coordinate stabilization and peacebuilding operations among civilian donors, now known as the International Stabilization and Peacebuilding Initiative (ISPI).[69] A coordinating body for support of national-level justice should follow the ISPI model as a nonbinding coordination mechanism. The CODA would be advisory, encouraging but not mandating field-level coordination, highlighting areas of neglect and duplication so that donors may wisely allocate their support. Coordination would take place on a country-specific basis, allowing different governments with varying levels of expertise to take the lead for coordinating support to particular countries while also paying significant deference to the desires of recipient governments. Involving national governmental and civil society leaders from countries in which the atrocities in question took place will be important for strengthening national ownership and making a long-term impact in those countries.

A coordinating body also would develop a database of donor efforts, thereby establishing a transparent routine for donors to determine who is doing what, so as to trigger coordination and avoid duplication. All participants would commit to reporting on their activities. Participants would share responsibility for particular domestic justice needs in individual countries (for instance, in the DRC, the United States could be responsible for investigative and prosecutorial training and education, Norway could be responsible for judicial reform and education, Germany could handle infrastructure, and so forth).[70]

Any coordinating body should not be the province of one government. Ideally, it would be based in a multilateral institution. The ICC and its Assembly of States Parties are not eager, funded, or qualified to take on a new and ambitious role to lead and coordinate the field. The UN's Rule of Law Coordination and Resource Group, if given an appropriate mandate, would be an appropriate model, but as a small bureaucratic group focused generally on the vast world of rule of law assistance, it is not now prepared for this kind of effort. That said, the United Nations would provide the best home for a CODA, which should be independent of other groups so as to maintain its focus on accountability for mass atrocities.

The secretary of state should outline a diplomatic agenda to broaden support for national-level accountability.

Just as the international tribunals resulted from major diplomatic initiatives, improved national-level accountability requires that the United States take the diplomatic lead. In that case, three specific elements of that agenda need to be addressed. First, the United States needs to obtain the buy-in of other donor governments and international organizations. Potential partners are ready for coordination and would likely follow the U.S. lead, as all donors are facing pressure to allocate assistance in efficient, results-oriented ways. Moreover, leading NGOs could be expected to assist in generating support, as many are pressing for better coordination and increased attention to the problems of supporting national processes.[71] The United States should involve leading governments in the area of international justice—such as Germany, the United Kingdom,

France, Scandinavian countries, Canada, South Africa, Japan, and the Netherlands—in preliminary consultations to launch a CODA.

Second, the United States and like-minded countries should create incentives for postconflict governments to establish domestic accountability. Some governments want to develop domestic mechanisms, as Bosnia did a decade ago, and only need the incentives of financial and technical assistance. Others, however, may lack the political will to launch such efforts, and external actors—individual governments and the Security Council—will need to encourage or pressure them to take responsible steps. That encouragement may take the form of positive inducements, such as the promise of access to aid or enhanced participation in international organizations. Positive inducements generated the desired responses in Serbia and Croatia, for instance, where domestic actors built war crimes processes with the prodding of the EU. Some situations, however, require more stick than carrot, such as in Burma/Myanmar and Sri Lanka, where governments are unwilling to address past behavior. International actors should condition political participation, nonhumanitarian assistance, and other forms of cooperation on the institution of domestic accountability for mass human rights abuses. External actors should be sensitive to *good faith* arguments about the importance of stability and peace. In those cases where investigation and prosecution are not immediately available, external actors should encourage responses to widespread human rights and humanitarian law violations that serve other valuable purposes. These may include inquiries and historical truth commissions, but the United States and others should generally not support processes that completely foreclose the later availability of criminal process.

Third, the United States and its partners should tap into regional forums. Regional courts have played a useful role in encouraging states to develop national accountability regimes. They are also repositories of expertise in the application of human rights norms within their regions. The United States and others should consider the creation of regional training centers for lawyers and judges, taught at the regional courts. Collaborating with American NGOs and universities, governments could pilot such a training center in a place such as Arusha, Tanzania, taking advantage of the expertise at the ICTR and the East African Court of Justice, and the Lagos-based Court of Justice of ECOWAS, to provide long-term education of lawyers and judges from countries in the region and its neighbors.

The United States should take short- and long-term steps to improve the likelihood that national processes will succeed.

Over the short term, the United States and other governments should identify those states that lack domestic laws to enable investigations and prosecutions for war crimes, crimes against humanity, and genocide. Donors should work with those states to draft appropriate legislation, an area in which the international community has substantial experience. Where appropriate, the United States should encourage governments in the midst of or emerging from conflict to develop specific expertise in handling international crimes, either through dedicated war crimes chambers or prosecutorial posts focused exclusively on such offenses. Even as Libya remains in conflict, the United States should initiate discussions with its allies to develop a plan for supporting national justice after the conflict, in the wake of a departure of the Qaddafi regime.

The United States should also propose a standby mechanism that collects and preserves evidence when a government is unable to do so. The United Nations now creates ad hoc teams to investigate and report on critical situations, such as the DRC Mapping Exercise. With its partners, the United States should press the UN Security Council to establish a permanent team of highly qualified and renowned experts ready to conduct the same kind of investigations, available to collect information when directed by the Security Council. Some governments are already thinking along these lines, having created Justice Rapid Response. But the Security Council would provide authority and credibility that individual governments cannot. The United Nations has already proven itself capable of organizing credible fact-finding missions and commissions of inquiry in cases as diverse as Lebanon, Sudan, the DRC, and many other places. A standby body of investigators capable of taking testimony, collecting evidence, and reporting to governments and the Security Council would preserve the ability of states to develop domestic accountability after conflict.

Over the long term, the United States and its partners should also support two important objectives. First, it should improve outreach to national communities. No process of postconflict national justice will be sustainable if it lacks the understanding and commitment of local governments and communities. The United States and others need to focus on the so-called demand side of justice.[72] In order to achieve the multiple goals of criminal justice, accountability processes need to educate national communities in ways that are understandable and reinforce basic international norms of human rights and the laws of war. But they cannot be short-term and one-off affairs. Outreach efforts should make concerted use of social media and other Internet and mobile technologies to broaden access to information about accountability.

Second, the United States should provide assistance for infrastructure, education, and sustainable training. Bosnia provides an example of how support for infrastructure makes a difference. The DRC, even if it wants to pursue domestic accountability, may be unable to do so until it enjoys the material foundation for justice—courts, offices, police stations, detention facilities, communication links, computers, vehicles, and other assets the developed world takes for granted. Infrastructure is costly, but it should be seen as an investment in institutions that contributes not only to accountability for the most serious crimes but also to general rule of law development.

Infrastructure development also applies to basic elements of security. The United States should link its security sector reform efforts to accountability, recognizing that effective law enforcement and courts—central elements of security and public safety—are essential to accountability as well. Weak or corrupt (or worse) police forces, an intimidating military or security services, and unchecked local violence usually disable investigations and prosecutions of mass atrocities. Similarly, focusing on prisons, police, and security services in the context of accountability can contribute to broader security reform. Strategies to support and develop security sectors need to take into account the role of national investigations and prosecutions in improving security and stability as well.

With respect to training, the United States should support those efforts that have a component of long-term education and mentorship, linking experts from developed countries or the international courts to professionals in developing countries over lengthy periods. Donors should develop university partnerships and exchanges in which students in a variety of fields related to accountability are provided with assistance to study abroad and in which faculty from foreign universities regularly teach in the developing system.

Conclusion

Nearly two decades after the UN Security Council initiated the era of international criminal tribunals, the United States and its partners should find ways to ensure that the products of those experiences—the jurisprudence, the procedural innovations, the creation of a professional class of international criminal lawyers—transfer to national investigations and prosecutions. Success could benefit not only the cause of justice but, if done right, stability and the rule of law more generally. Accountability at national levels presents great and varied challenges, as needs vary from country to country while donor dollars are growing scarcer. By beginning with some essential tools, however, governments may find ways to make their dollars and euros go further and their impact on national-level justice deeper and more effective than is currently the case. The United States, for so long a leader in international justice, should take on a leading role in the midst of this shifting landscape.

Endnotes

1. This report concerns war crimes, crimes against humanity, and genocide, i.e., those acts defined as criminal and subject to prosecution under international law. For present purposes, it excludes other crimes defined under international law, such as terrorism and piracy.

2. *World Development Report 2011: Conflict, Security and Development*, a report of the World Bank (April 2011), pp. 125–26, http://wdr2011.worldbank.org/sites/default/files/Complete%202011%20WDR%20Conflict%2CSecurity%20and%20Development_0.pdf.

3. See, generally, Human Rights Watch, "Selling Justice Short: Why Accountability Matters for Peace" (July 2009), http://www.hrw.org/node/84264.

4. According to "the Report of the Mapping Exercise documenting the most serious violations of human rights and international humanitarian law committed within the territory of the Democratic Republic of the Congo between March 1993 and June 2003": "Very few Congolese and foreign civilians living on the territory of the DRC managed to escape the violence, and were victims of murder, mutilation, rape, forced displacement, pillage, destruction of property or economic and social rights violations." August 2010, http://www.ohchr.org/Documents/Countries/ZR/DRC_MAPPING_REPORT_FINAL_EN.pdf, p. 8.

5. See especially "Putting Complementarity into Practice: Domestic Justice for International Crimes in the DRC, Uganda and Kenya," a report of the Open Society Justice Initiative (January 2011), pp. 18–57, http://www.soros.org/initiatives/justice/focus/international_justice/articles_publications/publications/complementarity-in-practice-20110119/putting-complementarity-into-practice-20110120.pdf.

6. The most cogent argument concerning the practical barriers facing international justice may be found in Jack Snyder and Leslie Vinjamuri, "Trials and Errors: Principle and Pragmatism in Strategies of International Justice," *International Security*, vol. 28, no. 3 (Winter 2003/04), pp. 5–44.

7. World Bank, *World Development Report 2011*, p. 2.

8. See Ruti Teitel, *Transitional Justice* (Oxford: Oxford University Press, 2000), pp. 28–29; and Jane Stromseth, David Wippman, and Rosa Brooks, *Can Might Make Rights?* (New York: Cambridge University Press, 2006), pp. 249–309.

9. On South Africa, see Robert I. Rotberg and Dennis Thompson, eds., *Truth v. Justice: The Morality of Truth Commissions* (Princeton: Princeton University Press, 2000). On East Timor, see *Can Might Make Rights?* at 285–89. Stromseth et al. argue that criminal trials and truth commissions can accomplish different but reinforcing objectives. For instance, "truth commissions are more likely than trials to be effective in compiling a comprehensive 'truth' that addresses the broader context of a conflict and provides a fuller account of the factors contributing to atrocities." Ibid, p. 256.

10. An early but illuminating discussion may be found at Neil Kritz, "Coming to Terms with Atrocities: A Review of Accountability Mechanisms for Mass Violations of Human Rights," *Law & Contemporary Problems*, vol. 59 (Autumn 1996), p. 127. On *gacaca*, see Philip Clark, *The Gacaca Courts, Post-Genocide Justice and Reconciliation in Rwanda* (New York: Cambridge University Press, 2010).

11. Colombia's leading civil society organizations often work in collaboration with international entities such as the UN High Commissioner for Human Rights, the Open Society Justice Initiative, and the International Center for Transitional Justice, among others. Interviews conducted by the author, in Bogotá, Colombia, January 17–20, 2011.

12. See United Nations Security Council document S/RES/827, May 25, 1993, http://www.icty.org/x/file/Legal%20Library/Statute/statute_827_1993_en.pdf.

13. See UN Security Council document S/RES/955, November 8, 1994, http://www.unictr.org/Portals/0/English/Legal/Resolutions/English/955e.pdf.

14. A useful and still pertinent overview of U.S. arguments for and against the Rome Statute may be found at CFR's *Toward an International Criminal Court?* (1999), http://i.cfr.org/content/publications/attachments/International_Criminal_Court.pdf. For its part, the United States has never joined nor signaled the possibility of joining the ICC, even though its policy toward the court has evolved in more supportive ways since 2005.

15. At the time of this writing, the ICC is investigating or prosecuting individuals from the Central African Republic, the Democratic Republic of Congo, Sudan, Uganda, Kenya, and Libya. The governments of Uganda, Central African Republic, and the DRC sought ICC prosecution through a process now known as self-referral. In each situation, the ICC prosecutor has made the case that the subject domestic system was unwilling or unable to pursue genuine investigations and prosecutions. Another nine situations are under preliminary examination—Afghanistan, Colombia, Ivory Coast, Georgia, Guinea, Palestine, Nigeria, Korea, and Honduras—though few of them are expected to lead to formal investigations and prosecutions, http://www.icc-cpi.int/Menus/ICC/Structure+of+the+Court/Office+of+the+Prosecutor.

16. An interesting study of the costs of various tribunals may be found at Rupert Skilbeck, "Funding Justice: The Price of War Crimes Trials" (2008), http://www.wcl.american.edu/hrbrief/15/3skilbeck.pdf.

17. See Luis Moreno Ocampo, "Address to the Assembly of States Parties, Ninth Session," December 6, 2010, http://www.icc-cpi.int/iccdocs/asp_docs/ASP9/Statements/ICC-ASP9-statements-LuisMorenoOcampo-ENG.pdf; similarly, the ICTY struggled to be a credible force in the absence of suspects in custody, a process that changed only when policies of NATO (and later, Serb) authorities made apprehension a priority. See, for example, Wesley K. Clark, *Waging Modern War* (New York: PublicAffairs, 2001), pp. 73, 92.

18. See, for example, Laurel E. Fletcher and Harvey M. Weinstein, "A World Unto Itself? The Application of International Justice in the Former Yugoslavia," in Eric Stover and Harvey M. Weinstein, *My Neighbor, My Enemy: Justice and Community in the Aftermath of Mass Atrocity* (Cambridge: Cambridge University Press, 2004), pp. 29–48.

19. See, for example, Yael Ronen, *Prosecutions and Sentencing in the Western Balkans* [Impact of International Courts on Domestic Criminal Procedures in Mass Atrocity Cases (DOMAC), February 2010], http://www.domac.is/media/domac/DOMAC-4-2010.pdf; Diane F. Orentlicher, "Shrinking the Space for Denial: The Impact of the ICTY in Serbia" (Open Society Justice Initiative, 2008), http://www.soros.org/initiatives/justice/focus/international_justice/articles_publications/publications/serbia_20080520; Diane F. Orentlicher, "That Someone Guilty Be Punished: The

Impact of the ICTY in Bosnia" (Open Society Justice Initiative, 2010), http://www. soros.org/initiatives/justice/focus/international_justice/articles_publications/ publications/that-someone-guilty-20100707.

20. ICC Prosecutor Luis Moreno-Ocampo has repeatedly stated his view that the ICC should be seen as a success where national accountability works, urging states to support "complementary" efforts at the national level. In his first speech as prosecutor, he identified "the first task of the prosecutor's office: make its best effort to help national jurisdictions fulfil their mission." See "Election of the Prosecutor: Statement of Mr. Moreno-Ocampo," April 22, 2003, http://www.icc-cpi.int/Menus/ICC/ Structure+of+the+Court/Office+of+the+Prosecutor/Reports+and+Statements/ Press+Releases/Press+Releases+2003/.

21. See generally Cesare P.R. Romano, André Nollkaemper, and Jann K. Kleffner, eds., *Internationalized Criminal Courts* (Oxford: Oxford University Press, 2004); and Laura A. Dickinson, "The Promise of Hybrid Courts," *American Journal of International Law*, vol. 95 (2003), pp.295–310.

22. See, for example, David Cohen, "Seeking Justice on the Cheap: Is the East Timor Tribunal Really a Model for the Future?" (August 2002), http://scholarspace.manoa. hawaii.edu/bitstream/handle/10125/3790/api061.pdf;jsessionid=60F4847BF737FF4B 47A4233C955B5FA7?sequence=1; and Tom Perriello and Marieke Wierda, "Lessons from the Deployment of International Justices and Prosecutors in Kosovo" (International Center for Transitional Justice, March 2006), http://www.ictj.org/static/Prosecutions/Kosovo.study.pdf.

23. See James A. Goldston, "No Justice in the Killing Fields," *International Herald Tribune*, April 26, 2011, available at http://www.nytimes.com/2011/04/27/opinion/27ihtedgoldston27.html; and "Recent Developments at the Extraordinary Chambers in the Courts of Cambodia" (Open Society Justice Initiative, December 2010), http://www. soros.org/initiatives/justice/focus/international_justice/articles_publications/publications/cambodia-report-20101207/cambodia-khmer-rouge-report-20101207.pdf.

24. Individuals may claim that a national government, within the jurisdiction of one of the courts, has denied their right to a remedy for a violation of a specific right (for example, the right to life or the prohibition against torture). See, for example, Article 13 of the European Convention on Human Rights and Article 25 of the American Convention on Human Rights. In turn, the European and inter-American courts have pressed for effective investigations and, where warranted, prosecutions to provide such remedies. See, for example, European Court of Human Rights, "Khashiyev & Akayeva v. Russia," App. Nos. 57942/00 & 57945/00, February 24, 2005, http://www.echr.coe. int.

25. The role of the IACHR is complex. See James L. Cavallaro and Stephanie Erin Brewer, "Reevaluating Regional Human Rights Litigation in the Twenty-First Century: The Case of the Inter-American Court," *American Journal of International Law*, vol. 102 (2008), pp. 768–827.

26. The first decision of the African Court of Human Rights was issued on March 25, 2011, against Libya. See Human Rights Watch, "Libya: African Rights Court Issues First Ruling Against a State," March 30, 2011, http://www.hrw.org/en/news/2011/03/30/ libya-african-rights-court-issues-first-ruling-against-state. For the human rights initiative among ASEAN nations, see http://www.aseanhrmech.org.

27. For a brief overview of the mobile courts, see the Open Society Justice Initiative's introduction at http://www.soros.org/initiatives/justice/focus/international_justice/ projects/gender-justice-court; along with its reporting from the courts by Chuck Sudetic, http://blog.soros.org/2011/04/congo-justice-the-defendants-arrive/.

28. See Ted Piccone, "The contribution of the UN's special procedures to national level implementation of human rights norms," *International Journal of Human Rights*, vol. 15 (February 2011), pp. 206–231.

29. For instance, the UN Mapping Exercise for the DRC, see supra note 4, established by the secretary general, provided impetus for discussions among the Congolese government, foreign governments, and the UN as to whether to establish a hybrid tribunal ("mixed chambers") to deal with the massive crimes committed in that period. It brought together highly qualified investigators and lawyers to collect evidence of atrocities between 1993 and 2003. The resulting report collected over 1,500 documents and more than 1,000 witness interviews. See Human Rights Watch, "Tackling Impunity in Congo: Meaningful Follow-up to the UN Mapping Report," October 1, 2010, http://www.hrw.org/node/93228.

30. A concise overview of challenges may be found at Cecile Aptel, "Domestic Justice Systems and the Impact of the Rome Statute: Discussion Paper," from the Consultative Conference on International Criminal Justice, September 9–11, 2009, http://www.internationalcriminaljustice.net/experience/papers/session7.pdf.

31. The Bosnian model, though a qualified success, has not led to a significant transfer of expertise throughout the state, entity, and cantonal court systems, nor has it helped trigger a wider social process of dealing with the legacy of the war. See Alejandro Chehtman, *Developing the Capacity of Bosnia and Herzegovina to Process War Crimes Cases: Critical Notes on a "Success Story,"* paper on file with author (2010); and David Tolbert and Aleksandar Kontic, "The International Criminal Tribunal for the former Yugoslavia: Transitional Justice, the Transfer of Cases to National Courts, and Lessons for the ICC," in Carsten Stahn and Göran Sluiter, eds., *The Emerging Practice of the International Criminal Court* (Leiden: Koninklijke Brill, 2009), p. 135.

32. See Amanda Lyons and Michael Reed Hurtado, eds., *Contested Transitions: Dilemmas of Transitional Justice in Colombia and Comparative Experience* (International Center for Transitional Justice, 2011). See especially Michael Reed Hurtado, "Transitional Justice Under Fire: Five Reflections on the Colombian Case," ibid., at 87. On the general conflict situation in Colombia, see the International Crisis Group's "President Santos' Conflict Resolution Opportunity," October 13, 2010, http://www.crisisgroup.org/en/regions/latin-america-caribbean/andes/colombia/034-colombia-president-santoss-conflict-resolution-opportunity.aspx.

33. Interviews conducted by the author in Bogotá, Colombia, January 17–20, 2011.

34. A number of observers in Bogotá see this as a major failure. Interviews conducted by the author, Bogotá, Colombia, January 17–20, 2011. The principal support from the United States in this sector involves the Department of Justice's Office of Overseas Prosecutorial Development, Assistance, and Training (OPDAT), which places DoJ lawyers in embassies around the world in order to provide dedicated, long-term training and assistance, http://www.justice.gov/criminal/opdat/. See also Department of Justice, Colombia Justice Sector Reform Program, Colombia Fact Sheet, January 2011. OPDAT lawyers in places as diverse as Colombia and Serbia have engaged in day-to-day support for host government officials working in the areas of accountability. They work with DoJ's International Criminal Investigative Training Assistance Program (ICITAP) to provide sustained assistance to investigators in a range of law enforcement situations.

35. One story circulating among NGOs in Bogotá tells of ICC prosecutor Luis Moreno-Ocampo, in a discussion with leading Colombian legal figures, including some from that country's supreme court, throwing up his hands and saying, "If you don't do it [prosecute those most responsible for international crimes], then I will!" Interviews

conducted by the author, Bogotá, January 17–20, 2011. See also "Remarks by the President of the Republic of Colombia, Juan Manuel Santos, at the Ninth Session of the Assembly of States Parties to the Rome Statute of the International Criminal Court," December 6, 2010, http://www.icc-cpi.int/iccdocs/asp_docs/ASP9/Statements/ICC-ASP9-statements-JuanManuelSantos-ENG.pdf.

36. See, for example, Inter-American Court of Human Rights, "Case of the 'Mapiripán Massacre' v. Colombia," Judgment of September 15, 2005 (Merits, Reparations and Costs), http://www.corteidh.or.cr/docs/casos/articulos/seriec_134_ing.pdf.

37. For a statement of U.S. support for accountability in Bangladesh, see Stephen J. Rapp, U.S. ambassador-at-large for war crimes issues, "Press Conference with Ambassador Stephen Rapp," Dhaka, Bangladesh, January 13, 2011, http://photos.state.gov/libraries/bangladesh/8601/2011%20Press%20Releases/Rapp_press_conference.pdf.

38. See Human Rights Watch, "Judging Dujail: The First Trial before the Iraqi High Tribunal," November 2006, http://www.hrw.org/en/reports/2006/11/19/judging-dujail.

39. Avocats Sans Frontières, "Case Study: The Application of the Rome Statute of the International Criminal Court by the Courts of the Democratic Republic of Congo" (2009), http://www.asf.be/publications/ASF_CaseStudy_RomeStatute_Light_PagePerPage.pdf.

40. Open Society Justice Initiative, "Putting Complementarity into Practice," p. 6.

41. See Stephen J. Rapp, U.S. ambassador-at-large for war crimes issues, remarks delivered November 21, 2010, at opening of the Nuremberg Trials Memoriam in Nuremberg, Germany, http://www.state.gov/s/wci/us_releases/remarks/151884.htm; Human Rights Watch, "Tackling Impunity in Congo: Meaningful Follow-up to the UN Mapping Report."

42. Sudan, of course, is not the sole example of refusal to hold officials accountable. The same is true in Myanmar, Afghanistan, and numerous other countries. For instance, emergency laws and political attitudes have foreclosed attempts to seek accountability in Sri Lanka. See Kishali Pinto-Jayawardena, "Post-War Justice in Sri Lanka: Rule of Law, The Criminal Justice System and Commissions of Inquiry," International Commission of Jurists, January 2010, http://www.icj.org/IMG/Sri_Lanka_COI_18.01.09-2.pdf.

43. See the Chatham House meeting summary report, "Filling One of the Gaps in International Justice: Justice Rapid Response," October 23, 2007, http://www.chathamhouse.org.uk/files/10082_il231007.pdf; and the Justice Rapid Response website http://www.justicerapidresponse.org/index.htm.

44. See the joint USAID/U.S. Department of Defense/U.S. Department of State publication "Security Sector Reform," February 2009, http://www.usaid.gov/our_work/democracy_and_governance/publications/pdfs/SSR_JS_Mar2009.pdf.

45. Author interview with NGO officials, in New York, Washington, and Bogotá, during December 2010 and January 2011.

46. As one study put it, "the rule of law can neither be created nor sustained unless most people in a given society recognize its value and have a reasonable amount of faith in its efficacy." Stromseth et al., *Can Might Make Rights?*, p. 310.

47. This estimate is based on the 25 percent share of the tribunals' budgets that the United States provides, based on its regular UN assessment. See "In the dock, but for what?" *Economist*, November 25, 2010, http://www.economist.com/node/17572645?story_id=17572645&fsrc=rss. Concrete figures for the ICTY may be found on the ICTY website at http://www.icty.org/sid/325, but the ICTR does not maintain a similar site for cost figures. For Sierra Leone figures, see the November 23, 2010, press release from the U.S. Department of State spokesman's office, "The U.S. Provides $4.5 Million to Fund Special Court for Sierra Leone Trial of Charles Taylor," http://www.state.gov/r/

pa/prs/ps/2010/11/151810.htm.

48. See Steven Woehrel, "Conditions on U.S. Aid to Serbia," Congressional Research Service Report for Congress, January 7, 2008, http://www.fas.org/sgp/crs/row/RS21686.pdf; Julie Kim, "Balkan Cooperation on War Crimes Issues," CRS Report for Congress, January 14, 2008, http://www.fas.org/sgp/crs/row/RS22097.pdf. On Cambodia, see United States Public Law 08-447, section 554(e), which bars funds to any Cambodia tribunal until the U.S. secretary of state certifies judicial independence and other characteristics, http://www.gpo.gov/fdsys/pkg/PLAW-108publ447/pdf/PLAW-108publ447.pdf.

49. See, for example, John B. Bellinger III, legal adviser, U.S. Department of State, "The United States and International Law," remarks at The Hague, Netherlands, June 6, 2007, http://2001-2009.state.gov/s/l/rls/86123.htm; Obama administration policy toward the ICC has been spelled out at Harold Koh, legal adviser, U.S. Department of State, "The Obama Administration and International Law," speech to American Society of International Law, March 25, 2011, http://www.state.gov/s/l/releases/remarks/139119.htm; Stephen Rapp, U.S. ambassador-at-large for war crimes issues, statement to the review conference of the International Criminal Court, June 1, 2010, http://www.state.gov/s/wci/us_releases/remarks/142520.htm; and Harold Koh and Stephen Rapp, "Briefing: U.S. Engagement with the ICC and the Outcome of the Recently Concluded Review Conference," June 15, 2010, http://www.state.gov/s/wci/us_releases/remarks/143178.htm.

50. National Security Strategy of the United States, May 2010, p. 48, http://www.whitehouse.gov/sites/default/files/rss_viewer/national_security_strategy.pdf.

51. See, for example, Marc Grossman, U.S. undersecretary of state for political affairs, "American Foreign Policy and the ICC," speech to the Center for Strategic and International Studies, May 6, 2002, http://www.amicc.org/docs/Grossman_5_6_02.pdf; and Stephen Rapp, "Statement of the United States of America," to the ninth session of the ICC's Assembly of States Parties, December 7, 2010, http://www.amicc.org/docs/ASP_Rapp_Statement_12072010.pdf.

52. National Security Strategy, p. 48. The U.S. delegation to the 2010 ICC Review Conference in Kampala, Uganda, reiterated this support, pledging "to support rule of law and capacity building projects which will enhance states' ability to hold accountable those responsible for war crimes, crimes against humanity and genocide," http://amicc.org/docs/Review_Conference_Pledges_by_the_US.pdf.

53. Human Rights Watch concluded that, "while non-Iraqi advisors provided by the US Embassy have been indispensable to the day-to-day functioning of the court, they have proved a poor substitute for the direct participation of international judges, counsel, and managers in the court." See Human Rights Watch, *Judging Dujail: The First Trial before the Iraqi High Tribunal*, p. 6.

54. United States Public Law 111-212, Section 1012, http://www.gpo.gov/fdsys/pkg/PLAW-111publ212/pdf/PLAW-111publ212.pdf.

55. See "Fact Sheet: U.S. Global Development Policy," published by the White House, September 22, 2010, http://www.whitehouse.gov/the-press-office/2010/09/22/fact-sheet-us-global-development-policy.

56. U.S. Department of State, "Leading Through Civilian Power: The First Quadrennial Diplomacy and Development Review (2010)," http://www.state.gov/documents/organization/153139.pdf.

57. Ibid.

58. This has become known as "positive complementarity," in which external forces seek to build domestic capacity so that the national jurisdiction may be willing and able to pursue investigations and prosecutions. See Assembly of States Parties of the

International Criminal Court, "Report of the Bureau on Stocktaking: Complementarity," ICC-ASP/8/51, March 18, 2010, http://www.icc-cpi.int/iccdocs/asp_docs/ASP8R/ICC-ASP-8-51-ENG.pdf; Review Conference of the Rome Statute of the International Criminal Court, "Stocktaking of international criminal justice, Draft Informal summary by the focal points," RC/ST/CM/1, June 22, 2010, http://www.icc-cpi.int/iccdocs/asp_docs/RC2010/RC-ST-CM-1-ENG.pdf.

59. The most comprehensive assessment of international justice capacity-building programs has been undertaken by the DOMAC Project, an international academic partnership, while others have undertaken detailed assessments of support in Kenya, the Democratic Republic of Congo, and Uganda. For the DOMAC material, see Alejandro Chehtman and Ruth Mackenzie, "Capacity Development in International Criminal Justice: A Mapping Exercise of Existing Practice," DOMAC/2, September 2009, http://www.domac.is/media/domac-skjol/DOMAC2-2009.pdf. See also International Criminal Court, "Focal points' compilation of examples of projects aimed at strengthening domestic jurisdictions to deal with Rome Statute Crimes," Review Conference of the Rome Statute, RC/ST/CM/INF.2, May 30, 2010, http://www.icc-cpi.int/iccdocs/asp_docs/RC2010/Stocktaking/RC-ST-CM-INF.2-ENG.pdf; Open Society Justice Initiative, "Putting Complementarity into Practice"; Avocats Sans Frontières, "Case Study: The Application of the Rome Statute of the International Criminal Court by the Courts of the Democratic Republic of Congo."

60. Open Society Justice Initiative, "Putting Complementarity into Practice," pp. 22–37.

61. See http://www.undp.org/cpr/we_do/security_reform.shtml.

62. Interview by author, United Nations official, New York, December 2010; interviews of senior NGO officials, New York, December 2010.

63. See Sang-Hyun Song, president of the ICC, "Keynote remarks at ICTJ retreat on complementarity," October 28, 2010, http://www.icc-cpi.int/NR/rdonlyres/01E1CD2E-8B10-4E67-83E3-011C499B49B9/282629/101028PresidentSong.pdf.

64. The World Bank concludes that donors "generally assess priorities and develop their programs separately, with efforts to help national reformers build unified programs the exception rather than the rule. . . . Aid is fragmented into small projects, making it difficult for governments to concentrate efforts on a few key results." *World Development Report 2011*, p. 25.

65. International Center for Transitional Justice, "Complementarity after Kampala: The Way Forward," November 19, 2010, p. 3, http://www.ictj.org/static/Publications/ICTJ_Complementarity_GreentreeSummary_Nov2010.pdf.

66. See, for example, James Goldston, "The Log in America's Eye," *International Herald Tribune*, December 21, 2010, http://www.nytimes.com/2010/12/22/opinion/22iht-ed-goldston22.html?ref=internationalcriminalcourt.

67. One senior official privately suggested that the U.S. government needs a state department bureau devoted solely to the subject of rule of law and accountability. Interview by author, Washington, DC, December 2010.

68. See, for example, Jonathan Fanton and Zachary Katznelson, "Human Rights and International Justice: Challenges and Opportunities at an Inflection Point," March 1, 2011 (paper on file with author).

69. See http://www.state.gov/s/crs/what/140119.htm.

70. Mark Ellis proposes the creation of an international technical assistance office to coordinate support for domestic justice. See Mark S. Ellis, "International Justice and the Rule of Law: Strengthening the ICC through Domestic Prosecutions," *Hague Journal on the Rule of Law*, vol. 1, no. 1 (2009), pp. 79–86.

71. The International Center for Transitional Justice, for instance, hosted a meeting of

sixty government, international organization, and NGO leaders on the subject of sup-
porting national justice in the fall of 2010. See International Center for Transitional
Justice, *Meeting Summary of the Retreat on "Complementarity after Kampala: The Way
Forward,"* November 19, 2010, paper on file with author.

72. I owe Jane Stromseth for the phrase "demand side" in this context. See Jane Stromseth, "Justice on the Ground: Can International Criminal Courts Strengthen Domestic Rule of Law in Post-Conflict Societies?" *Hague Journal on the Rule of Law*, vol. 1,
no. 1 (2009), pp. 87–97. ("Strengthening public demand and confidence in justice" is
crucial to sustainable rule of law building.)

About the Author

David A. Kaye is the executive director of the UCLA School of Law's international human rights program and director of its international justice clinic. He has taught courses in international law, international humanitarian law, and human rights at Georgetown University, Whittier Law School, and at the universities of Toulouse and Amsterdam. He has written extensively on international humanitarian law and the use of force. Before joining UCLA, Mr. Kaye served as an international lawyer with the U.S. State Department, serving as a legal adviser to the American embassy in The Hague, where he worked with the international criminal tribunals and acted as counsel to the United States in several cases before the International Court of Justice and the Iran-U.S. Claims Tribunal. From 1999 to 2002, he was the State Department's principal staff attorney on humanitarian law and served on several U.S. delegations to international negotiations and conferences. The State Department has honored him with four of its prestigious superior honor awards. Mr. Kaye is a member of the Council on Foreign Relations, the Executive Council of the American Society of International Law, and the Pacific Council on International Policy.

Advisory Committee for
Justice Beyond The Hague

This report reflects the judgments and recommendations of the author(s). It does not necessarily represent the views of members of the advisory committee, whose involvement in no way should be interpreted as an endorsement of the report by either themselves or the organizations with which they are affiliated.

Leila N. Sadat
Washington University

David J. Scheffer
Northwestern University School of Law

James B. Sitrick
Baker & McKenzie LLP

Jane E. Stromseth
Georgetown University Law Center

Ruti G. Teitel
New York Law School

David Tolbert
International Center for Transitional Justice

Allen S. Weiner
Stanford Law School

Council Special Reports

Published by the Council on Foreign Relations

The United States in the New Asia
Evan A. Feigenbaum and Robert A. Manning; CSR No. 50, November 2009
An International Institutions and Global Governance Program Report

Intervention to Stop Genocide and Mass Atrocities: International Norms and U.S. Policy
Matthew C. Waxman; CSR No. 49, October 2009
An International Institutions and Global Governance Program Report

Enhancing U.S. Preventive Action
Paul B. Stares and Micah Zenko; CSR No. 48, October 2009
A Center for Preventive Action Report

The Canadian Oil Sands: Energy Security vs. Climate Change
Michael A. Levi; CSR No. 47, May 2009
A Maurice R. Greenberg Center for Geoeconomic Studies Report

The National Interest and the Law of the Sea
Scott G. Borgerson; CSR No. 46, May 2009

Lessons of the Financial Crisis
Benn Steil; CSR No. 45, March 2009
A Maurice R. Greenberg Center for Geoeconomic Studies Report

Global Imbalances and the Financial Crisis
Steven Dunaway; CSR No. 44, March 2009
A Maurice R. Greenberg Center for Geoeconomic Studies Report

Eurasian Energy Security
Jeffrey Mankoff; CSR No. 43, February 2009

Preparing for Sudden Change in North Korea
Paul B. Stares and Joel S. Wit; CSR No. 42, January 2009
A Center for Preventive Action Report

Averting Crisis in Ukraine
Steven Pifer; CSR No. 41, January 2009
A Center for Preventive Action Report

Congo: Securing Peace, Sustaining Progress
Anthony W. Gambino; CSR No. 40, October 2008
A Center for Preventive Action Report

Deterring State Sponsorship of Nuclear Terrorism
Michael A. Levi; CSR No. 39, September 2008

China, Space Weapons, and U.S. Security
Bruce W. MacDonald; CSR No. 38, September 2008

Sovereign Wealth and Sovereign Power: The Strategic Consequences of American Indebtedness
Brad W. Setser; CSR No. 37, September 2008
A Maurice R. Greenberg Center for Geoeconomic Studies Report

Securing Pakistan's Tribal Belt
Daniel Markey; CSR No. 36, July 2008 (Web-only release) and August 2008
A Center for Preventive Action Report

Avoiding Transfers to Torture
Ashley S. Deeks; CSR No. 35, June 2008

Global FDI Policy: Correcting a Protectionist Drift
David M. Marchick and Matthew J. Slaughter; CSR No. 34, June 2008
A Maurice R. Greenberg Center for Geoeconomic Studies Report

Dealing with Damascus: Seeking a Greater Return on U.S.-Syria Relations
Mona Yacoubian and Scott Lasensky; CSR No. 33, June 2008
A Center for Preventive Action Report

Climate Change and National Security: An Agenda for Action
Joshua W. Busby; CSR No. 32, November 2007
A Maurice R. Greenberg Center for Geoeconomic Studies Report

Planning for Post-Mugabe Zimbabwe
Michelle D. Gavin; CSR No. 31, October 2007
A Center for Preventive Action Report

The Case for Wage Insurance
Robert J. LaLonde; CSR No. 30, September 2007
A Maurice R. Greenberg Center for Geoeconomic Studies Report

Reform of the International Monetary Fund
Peter B. Kenen; CSR No. 29, May 2007
A Maurice R. Greenberg Center for Geoeconomic Studies Report

Nuclear Energy: Balancing Benefits and Risks
Charles D. Ferguson; CSR No. 28, April 2007

Nigeria: Elections and Continuing Challenges
Robert I. Rotberg; CSR No. 27, April 2007
A Center for Preventive Action Report

The Economic Logic of Illegal Immigration
Gordon H. Hanson; CSR No. 26, April 2007
A Maurice R. Greenberg Center for Geoeconomic Studies Report

The United States and the WTO Dispute Settlement System
Robert Z. Lawrence; CSR No. 25, March 2007
A Maurice R. Greenberg Center for Geoeconomic Studies Report

Bolivia on the Brink
Eduardo A. Gamarra; CSR No. 24, February 2007
A Center for Preventive Action Report

After the Surge: The Case for U.S. Military Disengagement from Iraq
Steven N. Simon; CSR No. 23, February 2007

Darfur and Beyond: What Is Needed to Prevent Mass Atrocities
Lee Feinstein; CSR No. 22, January 2007

Avoiding Conflict in the Horn of Africa: U.S. Policy Toward Ethiopia and Eritrea
Terrence Lyons; CSR No. 21, December 2006
A Center for Preventive Action Report

Living with Hugo: U.S. Policy Toward Hugo Chávez's Venezuela
Richard Lapper; CSR No. 20, November 2006
A Center for Preventive Action Report

Reforming U.S. Patent Policy: Getting the Incentives Right
Keith E. Maskus; CSR No. 19, November 2006
A Maurice R. Greenberg Center for Geoeconomic Studies Report

Foreign Investment and National Security: Getting the Balance Right
Alan P. Larson and David M. Marchick; CSR No. 18, July 2006
A Maurice R. Greenberg Center for Geoeconomic Studies Report

Challenges for a Postelection Mexico: Issues for U.S. Policy
Pamela K. Starr; CSR No. 17, June 2006 (Web-only release) and November 2006

U.S.-India Nuclear Cooperation: A Strategy for Moving Forward
Michael A. Levi and Charles D. Ferguson; CSR No. 16, June 2006

Generating Momentum for a New Era in U.S.-Turkey Relations
Steven A. Cook and Elizabeth Sherwood-Randall; CSR No. 15, June 2006

Peace in Papua: Widening a Window of Opportunity
Blair A. King; CSR No. 14, March 2006
A Center for Preventive Action Report

Neglected Defense: Mobilizing the Private Sector to Support Homeland Security
Stephen E. Flynn and Daniel B. Prieto; CSR No. 13, March 2006

Afghanistan's Uncertain Transition From Turmoil to Normalcy
Barnett R. Rubin; CSR No. 12, March 2006
A Center for Preventive Action Report

Preventing Catastrophic Nuclear Terrorism
Charles D. Ferguson; CSR No. 11, March 2006

Getting Serious About the Twin Deficits
Menzie D. Chinn; CSR No. 10, September 2005
A Maurice R. Greenberg Center for Geoeconomic Studies Report

Both Sides of the Aisle: A Call for Bipartisan Foreign Policy
Nancy E. Roman; CSR No. 9, September 2005

Forgotten Intervention? What the United States Needs to Do in the Western Balkans
Amelia Branczik and William L. Nash; CSR No. 8, June 2005
A Center for Preventive Action Report

A New Beginning: Strategies for a More Fruitful Dialogue with the Muslim World
Craig Charney and Nicole Yakatan; CSR No. 7, May 2005

Power-Sharing in Iraq
David L. Phillips; CSR No. 6, April 2005
A Center for Preventive Action Report

Giving Meaning to "Never Again": Seeking an Effective Response to the Crisis
in Darfur and Beyond
Cheryl O. lgiri and Princeton N. Lyman; CSR No. 5, September 2004

Freedom, Prosperity, and Security: The G8 Partnership with Africa: Sea Island 2004 and Beyond
J. Brian Atwood, Robert S. Browne, and Princeton N. Lyman; CSR No. 4, May 2004

Addressing the HIV/AIDS Pandemic: A U.S. Global AIDS Strategy for the Long Term
Daniel M. Fox and Princeton N. Lyman; CSR No. 3, May 2004
Cosponsored with the Milbank Memorial Fund

Challenges for a Post-Election Philippines
Catharin E. Dalpino; CSR No. 2, May 2004
A Center for Preventive Action Report

Stability, Security, and Sovereignty in the Republic of Georgia
David L. Phillips; CSR No. 1, January 2004
A Center for Preventive Action Report

To purchase a printed copy, call the Brookings Institution Press: 800.537.5487.
Note: Council Special Reports are available for download from CFR's website, www.cfr.org.
For more information, email publications@cfr.org.